Each book in this series is a thematic collection of words children use, words they see around them, and words for objects with which they are familiar.

Very young children will enjoy talking about the pictures and naming the items. Older children will be able to use the books as reference for their reading and writing, as well as for enjoyment.

Titles in this series

Me and Other People

Everyday Things

At Home

Things That Move

Places to Go

Also available as a Gift Box set

LADYBIRD BOOKS, INC., Lewiston, Maine 04240 U.S.A.
© LADYBIRD BOOKS LTD MCMLXXXVII
Loughborough, Leicestershire, England
Printed in England

me
and other people

compiled by LYNNE BRADBURY
illustrated by TERRY BURTON

Ladybird Books

Girl

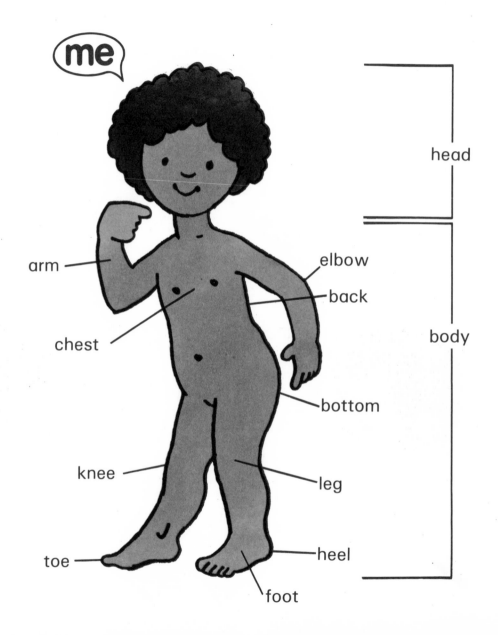

4

Boy

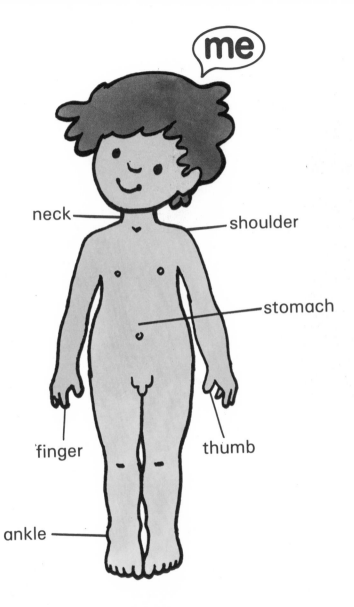

me

neck

shoulder

stomach

finger

thumb

ankle

Faces

hair

eyebrow

nose

chin

eye

mouth

ear

cheek

Indoor clothes

blouse

shirt

tie

skirt

jeans

undershirt

T-shirt

dress

pocket

socks

pants

sweater

cardigan

jacket

9

Outdoor clothes

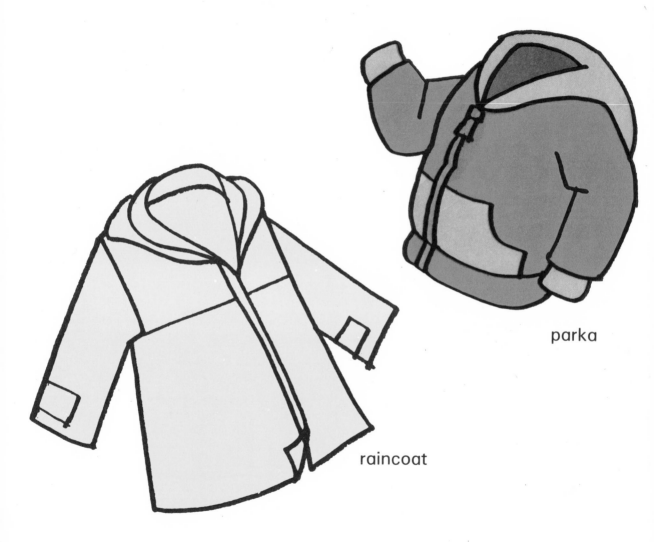

parka

raincoat

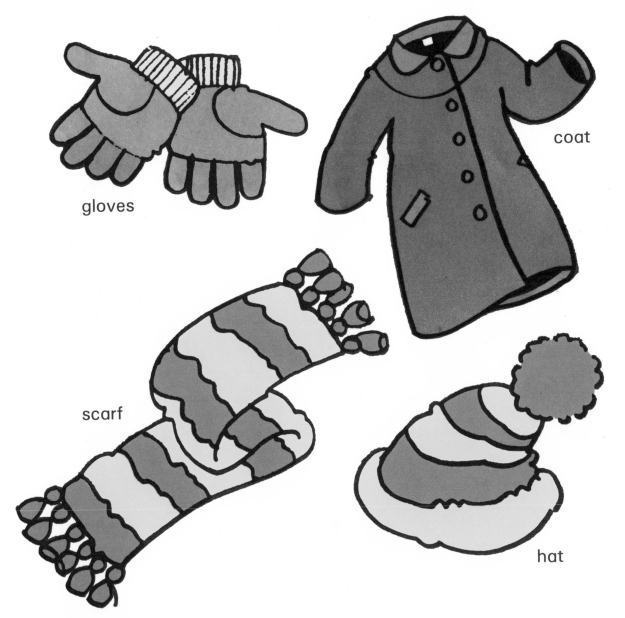

gloves

coat

scarf

hat

Night clothes

nightgown

pajamas

robe

slippers

Footwear

shoes

slippers

boots

sandals

sneakers

Family

aunt

mother/
mom/
mommy

baby

uncle

father/
dad/
daddy

brother

brother

sister

cousin

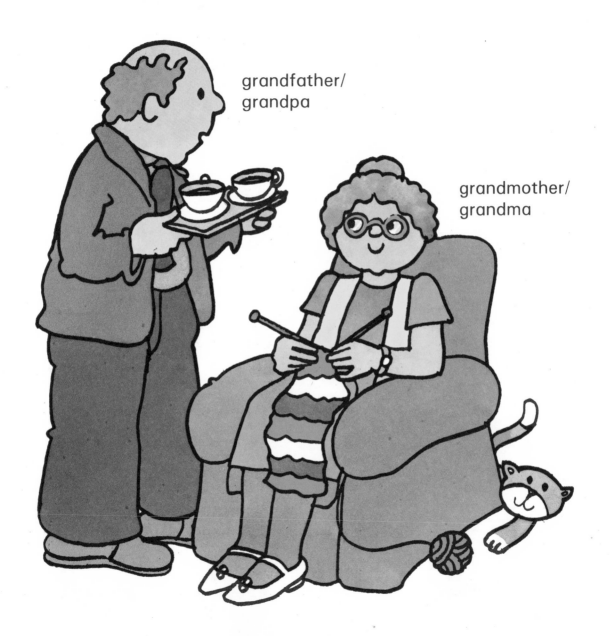

grandfather/
grandpa

grandmother/
grandma

Jobs

house painter

cook/chef

butcher

construction engineer

doctor

firefighter

19

factory worker

hairdresser

bus driver

miner

motorcycle police officer

nurse

police officer

mail carrier

sales clerk

teacher

6 + 2 =

scientist

waiter

waitress

Sportsmen and women

auto racing

skiing

boxing

motorcycle racing

wrestling

soccer

rugby football

parachuting

football

golf

cycling

baseball

ice skating

running

hurdling

horseback
riding

basketball

swimming

wind surfing

sailing

fishing

rowing

badminton

tennis

cricket

ice hockey

table tennis